The Soul School Music Memoirs

of Dr. Marshall Thompson of The Chi-Lites

Gumbo for the Soul Publications

The Soul School Music Memoirs
of Dr. Marshall Thompson of The Chi-Lites
Gumbo for the Soul Publications

Foreword by: Dr. Otis Williams

Dedication by: Beverly Black Johnson

Introduction by: Daisy Brown

Interior Layout and Cover Design: Big Easy Creative

©2023 Gumbo for the Soul Publications
www.gumboforthesoulinternational.com

Order Direct
www.soulschoolmusic.org
thatsoulschoolmusic@gmail.com

ISBN: 979-8-218-26283-9

Produced and Printed in the United States of America
10 9 8 7 6 5 4 3 2

Foreword

By Dr. Otis Williams

The *Soul School Music Memoirs of Marshall Thompson* is more than an account of an extraordinary music legend, it is a singular chronicle of American R&B/soul music history with roots in Chicago, Illinois. It's the legendary singer, songwriter, Marshall Thompson's story, as only he can tell it.

I have always loved the harmonies and songs of The Chi-Lites. Their famous chart hits such as "Have You Seen Her," "Oh Girl," and "Are You My Woman (Tell Me So)," are among some of the greatest recordings of Chicago's R&B/soul sound from the 70s. These mega hits by The Chi-Lites, and many others, are now a part of popular music worldwide.

Thompson, a founding member of The Chi-Lites, and I, a founding member of The Temptations have some things in common. We have both traveled on a journey of a lifetime. We are among the "last men standing," the sole remaining founding members of trailblazing male vocal groups from the 60s. Our endurance has earned us recognition as torch bearers of cherished music catalogs passed between generations and celebrated worldwide. This has all been made possible by the Grace of God.

We are both blessed to be part of world-famous vocal groups, whose multitude of iconic voices will always be a part of our history. And now, as our respective groups tour around the world and record new music in the 21ˢᵗ century, our current lineups are continuing to reach new generations. As entertainment insiders, Marshall and I can attest to the power of music. We love performing because music can bring people together from all walks of life. We've seen music become in the 60s, and even today, like a soothing ointment for a troubled world.

Looking back over our careers, I realize the love of music was in our hearts from an early age. In my youth, I remember the rousing gospel music filling the pews in my grandmother's Black Baptist church in Texarkana, Texas. In my grandmothers' home, the sounds of the Dixie Hummingbirds, the Soul Stirrers and Mahalia Jackson filled the house, along with the sweet smell of her hot water bread cooking on the stove, as she sang aloud in the kitchen. Those memories last a lifetime.

At a young age, Marshall must have felt that same intensity, that same force of nature taking hold in his life that I felt as a teenager in Detroit. Being surrounded by extraordinary musical talent, Marshall in Chicago, and me in Detroit, was inspiring for us. Influenced by his father, William Thompson, who performed in famous theaters and dinner clubs in the country, Marshall found his own voice, and with other locally sourced singers from Chicago, formed The Chi-Lites. The rest is history.

I was fortunate enough to be a part of one of the greatest music labels in American popular culture, Motown, out of Detroit, Michigan. In the 60s and 70s, epic R&B/soul music was also being recorded in cities across the country, such as Chicago, Philadelphia, Memphis, Los Angeles, and New York.

Marshall and I first met when The Temptations and other Motown artists were on our Motortown Revue tours in the 60s. We came through Chicago to perform at the pre-eminent Regal Theater located then in the Southside of the city. We, and the other Motown entertainers, would stop and eat near the theater, and during one of those occasions, we ("the Classic Five" lineup) met Marshall. At that time, little did we know The Chi-Lites would soon become superstars too. Recently, Marshall told me how much The Temptations' music and dazzling concert performances inspired them and many other artists during that era.

We both have so much to be thankful for, including our beloved chart hits, numerous awards, and honors. Congratulations to Marshall and the group on receiving a star on the legendary Hollywood Walk of Fame in 2021. They are also inductees of the Rhythm and Blues Foundation, the R&B Music Hall of Fame, and the Vocal Group Hall of Fame.

Having published my life story, *Temptations,* which was sourced for the smash hit, Tony Award-winning Broadway musical, *Ain't Too Proud: The Life and Times of The Temptations*, currently on tour across the country, I came to realize the importance of introspection. Sharing our personal stories with the world is significant for historical record.

Speaking from experience, I can say that readers interested in American culture, particularly an insider's view of music history, will find Marshall's memoir is a reading journey worth taking. It's a master class in the history of R&B/soul music, Chicago style.

We thank our fans everywhere. God Bless You All.

See Ya Later, Gone!

~ Dr. Otis Williams,
Founding Member, The Temptations

Soul School Music

Dedication

By Beverly Black Johnson

I have been truly honored to carve out my own niche as the curator of some of the greatest conversations with legendary musicians and singers from all around the world. The Soul School Music of Dr. Marshall Thompson, The Chi-Lites' last living original member started out by a chance meeting with him. He agreed to partner with me as Co-hosts to take this musical journey to another level on TRIBE Family Channel™ via internet radio under the brand of Soul School Music.

For the first 2 years straight, as a team, I would follow The Godfathers' mentoring and schedule interviews with some of the world's most widely known and esteemed entertainers, that has now spanned over a 6 year period, comprised of six seasons.

I am forever grateful to The Godfather, for believing in greater possibilities through our collective abilities to work together as a class-act. Taking the time to mentor me will be a special part of this priceless journey forever etched in my soul. Never in life could I have ever imagined I'd be in the "cat-birds seat" listening to the gems drop from the very artists whose music I grew up listening to, moreover getting the chance to thank them for their music, exceeds my wildest dreams. These curated conversations down memory lane have become timeless treasures, and we are still enjoying who we can, while we can.

The ***Soul School Music Memoirs of Dr. Marshall Thompson*** are bits and pieces of memorable moments reminiscing on where, and how our guest artists met The Last Man Standing of The Chi-Lites. I hope you will enjoy them as much as I have.

With that said, this book is dedicated to you, the Soul School Music fans around the world.

Soulfully Yours,

~ Beverly

Introduction

By Daisy Brown

Looking back – the year 1971, the place was the Baltimore Civic Center. What a fantastic show! Many legendary groups appeared – Gladys Knight and the Pips, Al Green and, of course, The Chi-Lites, among many others. The event was a fundraiser. What a night of outstanding music it was. I was working at WEBB Radio Station at the time. With me being a lover of music, this job was perfect.

I was so excited to be able to meet these famous artists face-to-face. At the end of the evening I chauffeured Squirrel of The Chi-Lites to dinner and then to the hotel. He shared some of their travel stories with me and promised to stay in touch. The next day before leaving Baltimore, we met for breakfast. Wow! If only you could imagine the excitement of living a dream come true. But that was only the beginning.

A life-lasting friendship was born. I was adopted into The Chi-Lites family. I now have 4 big brothers who welcomed me into the world of music. Marshall "MT" Thompson was the group leader. The other members were Eugene "Gene" Record (1940-2005), Robert "Squirrel" Lester (1942-2010) and Creadel "Redd" Jones (1940-1994).

Being on the road with The Chi-Lites was now more than a dream come true. Meeting these four guys changed my life forever.

My big brother MT took me by the hand and spoon-fed me. Always a lover of music I now had first-hand teaching of the ins and outs of this wonderful world of music. MT was always willing to share his knowledge and experiences with anyone who asked. He eagerly advises newcomers to make it in the music industry the policy is "90% business, 10% show". Dedication and determination are necessary components as well.

His professional music career began as a drummer. His number one love, however, was to sing and dance. As the founding member of The Chi-Lites history was made. Under his leadership and the unseamed harmony, he spearheaded his great group's name to become a household name. and its music fluttered the airwaves. He wears many hats – The Godfather of Vocal Groups, The Last Man Standing of The Chi-Lites, The Chairman of Vocal Groups (Brunswick Records).

On September 30, 2021, on behalf of The Chi-Lites, he was the proud recipient of a Star on the Hollywood Walk of Fame (Star #2702). On August 24, 2022, MT celebrated his 80th birthday. The rewards and awards continued. October 16, 2022, The Chi-Lites Featuring Marshall Thompson established residency at the luxurious all-suites Rio Hotel and Casino in Las Vegas, NV. MT was also presented with an Honorary Doctorate of Philosophy in Humanitarianism from the Leaders Esteem Christian Bible University in Texas, only surpassed by a President's Lifetime Achievement award from President Biden.

What a joyous day of celebration! It is with great pride and pleasure to now make the name change from "MT" to "Dr. T" as he celebrates over 60 years in show business, touring and wowing his audiences worldwide.

It is a true honor and privilege to introduce this extraordinary composition envisioned by Beverly Black Johnson. It depicts the respect, memories and rapport established between Dr. T and many of his fellow artists and musicians.

This compilation will take you down memory lane via interviews with many fellow artists. This legendary group, led by Marshall Thompson, continues to impact the music industry. Being from a musical family, it was easy for him to follow in their footsteps. Always a performer, Marshall demands perfection from his band members, and what a show you would get. The Chi-Lites' music, penned by late lead vocalist Eugene Record, will live forever.

MT and I often relive highlights of travel, meeting the many die-hard fans and, of course, how much we miss Gene, Squirrel and Red. May they 'Rest in Paradise.' Our love for them and their contribution to the music is never-ending.

I know you will enjoy this phenomenal masterpiece!!!

~ Daisy Brown

Soul School Music

Praise Page

"As Dr. Marshall Thompson's personal friend and attendant of over 30 plus years, I have seen The Chi-Lites go from "Have You Seen Her?" to receiving a star on the Hollywood Walk of Fame and a Presidential Lifetime Achievement Medal in the entertainment field of music.

He always felt like he could throw a rock and hit the next show as we traveled down those long, lonely roads. He preached that we should always Shine at Your Brightest Light and watch the blessings come true for you.

As a child he believed in Holding On To His Dreams and is now in residency at the famous Rio Hotel and Casino.

The roads traveled weren't always easy, but he made it work!"

~ Kevin Jones

Soul School Music

Editor's Note

For the sake of continuity, and the ease of reading this book, we will not be using all the names of the players, but only that of Marshall Thompson and our radio show guests. We would again like to thank our generous team to these excerpts from the radio station broadcasts that comprise this book, for making it all possible, as follows:

Dr. Marshall Thompson (Co-Host)

Beverly Black Johnson (Creator, Co-Host)

Daisy Brown (Producer)

Gwen Nicks (Sponsor)

From each episode, we have gleaned the conversations for where the artists first met and some of their most memorable moments and standout reflections of then-and-now, to give you the most out of these pleasurable soul strolls down memory lane.

The shows are highlighted by order of appearance.

Be sure to get all 6 book in the series.

Full audio and documentary products are forthcoming.

Soul School Music

Table of Contents

Enjoy This Soulful Journey…

Soul School Music

AS BROADCASTED LIVE ON
TRIBE Family Channel™

Co-Host, Beverly Black Johnson introducing Host, Marshall Thompson on 1st show.

♪ ♪ ♪

Guests:
Brenda Lee Eager and Gary Dennis Hines, honoring Prince, The Artist.

Gary Hines:

Prince and I attended the same Junior High School. He could play hoop despite his height. He loved sports and he would want everyone to know he loved God. He would call to talk about God, music, and love. He was always very supportive of other artists. He would be at our shows but he'd be in the sound booth because he didn't want to cause a disruption. Every now and then he'd get up on stage with other artists. He took being supportive very seriously.

Marshall Thompson:

"Upon meeting Prince at Warner Brothers, I was amazed at the talent he had. He asked me to come to Minneapolis to perform for the neighborhood. I was honored. He was at a club in Australia when he heard The Chi-Lites' song "Bottoms Up!" and had planned to record it. We were like "Whoa!" We had a tour with The Whispers and we played at Radio City Music Hall. We had to come up with something funky, so we came up with Bottoms Up!"

Brenda Lee Eager:

"Prince was doing an album with Mavis Staples, and a year later I received a call from Mavis requesting some lyrics of mine so I sent a bunch of songs. Prince changed a couple of lines in the song and asked me if it was ok. It was such an honor. I'm deeply grieving for him. I am honored to have two songs recorded by him. He gave me a huge advance and didn't even know if the song was going to go platinum. He bought me my first baby grand piano."

Guest:
Sonny Turner

Sonny Turner:

I give all praise to people like yourselves (Beverly Black – Co-host and creator of Soul School Music) who keep artists like myself, Marshall, and different groups that made their contribution to music, alive and spreading it to a new generation. We are the ones bowing down in thankfulness, not only to God but to you all who are instrumental in helping us maintain, so thank you. It's my pleasure; I feel honored.

I was born in Fairmont, West Virginia and I was raised in Cleveland, Ohio, home of the Rock 'n Roll Hall of Fame; is that amazing!?

I have to give all praise to God and to my mother, who was a gospel singer, and members of the family who had musical abilities. My father was a welterweight boxing champion but my mother was a singer. She was the "music" in the family.

She raised us in church. We, of course, had to go to Sunday School. She sang in the choir and subsequently put me in the Junior Choir, and my brother too! That's where my roots come from; my musical roots come from her and so that's how I got started.

I loved music. Going to school, I sat by the radio during my growing up years emulating performers like Nat King Cole, the great Louis Armstrong, Roy Hamilton, just so many great black performers, artists and singers. Billy Holiday, you're talkin' Nina Solomon back in the days of Count Basie and Earl Garner, Duke Ellington, Sarah Vaughn, Dinah Washington, I mean on and on and on, ya' know. That's how I grew up, listening to that music, listening to the radio, and then getting interested with friends and fellow students who loved the same music.

We got involved with the little Doo Wop groups, we formed our little Doo Wop group and I just asked to join a group called "The Metro Tones", to make a long story short.

They had heard about this little guy that could sing a little bit. A couple of those guys were drafted into the service and they needed a lead singer and asked me to come to the rehearsal. We all knew the music that was current at the time, The Moonglows, The Flamingos, The Five Keys, etc, so were all familiar with all those beautiful songs and groups. They had a repertoire of all these different groups in their "stage" repertoire. I went to their rehearsal and they liked the way I sang and oddly enough, here's something else I can give you an idea to the spiritual guide to my career. There were four guys and a girl-now that was the format of The Platters. Unknowingly, we loved The Platters music and oddly enough there we were singing Platters' songs in our Doo Wop group. That was during the 50's.

Marshall Thompson:

That's some great talk right there! How're you doing?

I remember you from a long time ago, my buddy.

Sonny Turner:

Brother Marshall, it's a pleasure!

So here we are. Our destiny has come full circle, I think?

Marshall Thompson:

Right! We're Blessed to be here to do what we're doing. We have a great show here.

Sonny Turner:

I'm a longtime admirer of The Chi-lites, I'm telling you right now, and that song you were playing, "The Coldest Days of My Life" and everything else that you've recorded. It's so many of our fellow musicians and performers out here living in Vegas, and we have comradery with Glady's Knight, Bubba Knight, Lamonte McClemore of The Fifth Dimension, Little Anthony and The Imperials, Harry Elston, Leader of The Friends of Distinction, I could go on and on.

Marshall Thompson:

Wow. Yeah, I was drummer for Gladys Knight right before I started The Chi-lites, '58. '59, '60, I was right there playing for Gladys Knight at the Regal Theater.

Sonny Turner:

Is that right!? Wow, see there you go! I think were tied to one another spiritually, and as time goes by we have a chance to interact with one another, ya know.

Marshall Thompson:

You all are a great group; we loved all the songs that you had. Y'all just had some great, great songs and you know, I grew up on that. The bass singer was a very good friend of mine. Y'all were one of the greatest groups that has ever been on a microphone.

Sonny Turner:

Well, like you all, we've played to royalty, to dignitaries and we played to major audiences, Cricket Field; we even played to bull rings; different places in Spain, France, and all over Europe, and the Queen of England. You and I have tasted the highest realm of entertainment and here we still are.

Marshall Thompson:

We were all Blessed; we went to Greenland and I don't know too many people that has played in Greenland.

Sonny Turner:

I remember Greenland. My oldest brother was in the Air Force and he was stationed there.

Marshall Thompson:

Wow. Now that gig was something else. We'd go in there for one week. They had a plane that goes out once a week and you had to stay there a whole week before you could get back out of there.

Sonny Turner:

Isn't that something? And we're talking about the day turning into nighttime and night into day.

Marshall Thompson:

You better believe it! Scared me to death. I said when is it going to be light out?

Sonny Turner:

Six months of darkness! You were successful in what you were doing and I think that's why people sought after the group and the music and I know that's a wonderful experience that you fully enjoyed.

Guest:
Brenda Lee Eager

Brenda Lee Eager:

This is my Chicago brother. Loving you, man.

Marshall Thompson:

How're you doing? You've been loving us for so many years and we're all loving you.   I know you've listed all those that you performed with but don't forget them Chi-Lites!   You rode on that bus called "Oh Girl!"

Brenda Lee Eager:

Sure did. We'll talk about that. I started singing when I was three and by the time I got to the 3rd grade I was putting songs together. In the 9th grade I had my own group. When I grew up I took my first gig in Mobile, Alabama at a place called The Kings Club. I lied about my age, yes I did! I told them I was 18, when I was 17, but I was almost 18! I started singing for $40 a night, 2 nights a week!

I always say, start from the beginning. Learn as much as you can about this business and work it! Practice! Practice! Practice!

Marshall Thompson:

You better believe it! And we did The California Club for $25.00 dollars a night, me and The Whispers.

Brenda Lee Eager:

I didn't have the nerve to ask the band to do any songs that I had written, so I would do covers. One of the first persons I used to cover was Gladys Knight. I covered Aretha, Sarah Vaughn and Mahalia Jackson. These women really taught me: Gladys, Mavis, Aretha, Mahalia and Sarah Vaughn. I would just listen to those women and their voices and I just went to school studying them. Later on it was Ella Fitzgerald and other people like Dionne Warwick. Pops Staples once made me a Staple Singer. But before that at age 18, I went to New York and went to the Apollo Theater. I told my Mother I was going and she said, "Well, God's there too!" They wouldn't let me in to the Apollo so I wound up working at a sweat shop adding rhinestones to all the dresses that the women in show business wore.

When I Went back to Mobile my husband said we're moving to Chicago, and I was like Yay!   I was only 20 years and I loved Chicago. This is around 1967 and I joined Operation Breadbasket and became a soloist in the choir. Jesse Jackson took me and three other girls and made a group out of us called The Piperettes. We toured with Jesse, a 16 piece band with Tim Galloway, Hobie, and Ben Branch. Dr. King Jr. called Ben his favorite musician and told Ben the night before he died, "I want you to play 'Precious Lord', Ben. I want you to play it like you've never played before."

Marshall Thompson:

My cousin was the drummer with you all then, Terry Thompson, my Daddy's brother.

Brenda Lee Eager:

Yeah, that's right, your first cousin! We traveled all over the country getting people out to vote. We were instrumental in getting people elected singing on flatbed trucks out in the rain, marching in the snow. We did that work and we're very proud of that work. Jesse's brother Chat said we should write a song together, so we did. We wrote 'It's a Thrill, What I Feel' and he took it to Jerry Butler who liked the singers and the song. That's how my career started with Jerry and the second song was, 'Ain't Understanding Mellow'. In the rhythm section was Phil Upchurch and Donny Hathaway and some great musicians. That piano you're hearing on 'Ain't Understanding Mellow' is Donny Hathaway.

Marshall Thompson:

I think they had Maurice White on the drums.

Brenda Lee Eager:

I was holding little Lalah Hathaway in my arms when Donny went in to do his part. We did that song one time, in one take.

Marshall Thompson:

That's the same way we did 'Oh Girl'.

♪ ♪ ♪

Guest:
Little Anthony of Little Anthony and The Imperials

Little Anthony:

I've been singing since I was three. My mom was a gospel singer, my dad was a jazz musician; he played in the big bands, Buddy Johnson's Orchestra. All my Aunts were singers, and all of them were church singers. All of them came out of the Baptist church so I had that kind of influence in me from day one. All I heard in our house was music, constantly. My mother told me I started holding the right notes at three years old. My tonation was good but I didn't know what I was doing. Evidently she heard it and my Aunts would say, "You know what? That boy can sing!" So that's always been a part of me. I don't ever remember not singing; somewhere, somehow.

I ended up with different little groups and gospel groups; then I ended up with a group called 'The Duponts' out of high school. William Dockety, Bracy, Williams; I can't remember it was so long ago but we got together and started singing out of high school. The next thing you knew I got a shot at a record company called Wingley, which was an independent company in those days; there were a million of them. So that was my first time hearing my voice on the radio, way born to a professional studio. It came to me that this is what I wanted to do but I had no idea how far I could go, I was

27

just doing it. Just like everybody else was doing it! I had my favorite groups and singers; three of the groups that I loved so much was The Flamingos, The Minglos and The Dells. All these people were very influential to me, especially The Flamingos.

Then I left high school and The Duponts. Clarence Collins, one of the co-founders of The Imperials called me. Also, Earnest was one of the founders of a group called Chesters, but this was really The Imperials. They just changed our name. The group broke up, then came back together; it was crazy! They changed our name at the record company because they didn't like it. The next thing you know, they came up with this song called, 'Tears on my Pillow' and I didn't particularly like it, it didn't sound right because I was R&B and this was more Pop, so I had to deal with that. That was the beginning. "Tears on my Pillow' came out in 1958, I was 17 years old and the next thing I knew is I was a celebrity. It just kept going and going and going. We had ups and downs; I'm sure Marshall can testify to that.

The group broke up and came back together and broke up. It was crazy. Then what happened is we got a call from a nightclub owner by the name of Marti Gunty. He told my manager at the time, Ernie Martinelli, "I want you guys to come back together, and come to my club in Brooklyn ." We went in there and that was the beginning of a new era for us, because out of that we met Teddy Rondazo, Bobby Weinstein, Bobby Hart, and Don Kosner. DCP Records actually told us they had some songs they wanted us to hear and we'd like to sign you. And they did. The first tune we came out with on that label was, I'm on the Outside Looking In. Then came Hurt So Bad, Going Out of My Head, Take Me Back, Miss You So; it was just one hit after another.

As far as church, I did everything. I was with my Mama all the time. She was a Nazareth Baptist singer. That's how I met Sam Cooke. Sam Cooke used to come to my Aunt's house to stay when he'd come to New York. He called her Mrs. Ford. At that time he was with a group called The Soul-Stirrers, and he wasn't Sam Cooke yet -like we knew in the Pop world. It was just some wonderful times, man.

Marshall Thompson:

Wow. Right! Right! We basically went through the same situations, Anthony, but what I want to find out is when did you guys first go out on The Chittlin' Circuit like we did?

Little Anthony:

Well, we were the Pioneers. I feel sorry for y'all because you came behind us. (Laughs) It was rough! It was a point when I thought, this isn't what I thought show business was gone be like. You see, 75% of our gigs were down south during Jim Crow and segregation; and I wasn't used to that! I'm from Brooklyn! I mean there's all kinds of prejudices but it was very subtle. When I got down there I couldn't believe what was happening to me and the guys in the group! I said what the??? Colored fountains, and you can't sit here and you can't sit there; you can't do that and you can't go to the store. All kinds of crazy stuff. Finally, I called my mother who's from Savannah, Georgia. I said Mom, I'm coming home. I quit! I don't want to do this no more. My Mother, bless her heart, told me no, I come from the South. You gotta stand your ground! You've got to deal with it. This is what you do. You not going to always be in the south, but this is what you have to do. But all through I learned a lot; that I got to meet some wonderful people on the way. I met Ali, and I know you Ali. I met Rev. Dr. Martin Luther King, Rev. Abernathy, and on and on through all that mess. They encouraged us saying "Don't leave, keep doing what you're doing."

Marshall Thompson:

Yeah, I did too! Ali was our first manager.

♪ ♪ ♪

Guest:
Lamont McClemore
of The Fifth Dimension

Lamonte McClemore:

How are you Mr. Marshall Thompson? I want to wish you a very, very Happy Birthday cause you've always been one of my idols and I've always wanted to grow up to be just like you.

Marshall Thompson:

(Laughs) Well, hey man. It's always a pleasure to hear you say that; and you know I'd like to be like a whole lot of people I've known all my life, ya' know what I mean, and it's a blessing to be here.

Lamonte McClemore:

They say you can't add days to your life, but you can add life to your days, brother and I think that's what you and I have both done.

Marshall Thompson:

You better believe it!

Lamonte McClemore:

I want to thank you for inviting me and especially those behind the scenes making this possible, like Miss Beverly Black. One of these days it will be her. Where do you live now Marshall?

Marshall Thompson:

Right on! Right on!

Lamonte McClemore:

Marshall, where do you live now?

Marshall Thompson:

I still live in Chicago, Illinois in the Frankfort area.

Lamonte McClemore:

Oh, for some reason I kept thinking you had a place here in Vegas. I sure hope to see you soon. If you ever come this way you'll always have a Bar-B-Que sandwich and a Fish-fry waiting on you so c'mon.

Marshall Thompson:

I got so many friends out there, you know. Me and Joe Jackson are very close and my film company, Darryl Payne, is out there. I am out there quite a bit.

Lamonte McClemore:

I just went to Joe Jackson's birthday party last month.

Marshall Thompson:

I would have made it out there too, but I was on the road. He had a fabulous birthday party out there.

Lamonte McClemore:

I have a joke book out called, Everybody Loves A Good Dirty Joke, and the "good" is scratched out replaced with "Please Don't Buy This Book because It Talks About You and Yo' Mama!"

(Laughs). I also have out "From Hobo Flats to the Fifth Dimension" both are on Amazon.

This one is not a joke. Donald Trump was here in Las Vegas about three weeks ago; he was campaigning out of an Indian Reservation. He told the Indians, if y'all help make me president I'll get some of your property back on the reservation, put you on welfare and everything. So they were son impressed with Trump's speech they said, well we're going to give you an Honorary Indian Name, Walking Eagle. He said, oh great and when he walked back on his plane he told all the aids, the speech went great and they gave me an Honorary Name, Walking Eagle, but Indian names usually mean something. Can you look it up and see what it means? The aid came back and said, yeah, it means, Walking Eagle is so full of shit, he can't fly! (Laughs)

Marshall Thompson:

(Laughs) I got to put you on stage with me.

Lamonte McClemore:

I don't do anymore stand ups. I'll do some sit-downs! (Laughs)

Marshall Thompson:

It all started for me with Glady's Knight, my career, at The Regal Theater. What happened was I went down with my snare drum to audition. I had been rehearsing the song, Everybody Needs Love, for about three weeks before she got there. The house drummer couldn't play their music and I was sitting in the audience so I raised my hand because she said somebody's got to come up here and play my music. They only had three hours before showtime. I went up there and played that music and got the job, but when the curtains opened up, I froze up! I had never seen that many people in a theater! All my people in the family were out there in the audience looking at me, my mother, father, all the people in the audience was looking at me. All the kids were there from around the house and the school. I had told all of them around 42nd and King's Dr. that I was going to be at The Regal Theater playing with Gladys Knight. They thought I was nuts so when they saw me up there, they just went wild, and I froze. I couldn't do nothing. (Laughs)

Bubba told me to play like I did at sound check so when the second show opened up, I was wailing on those drums! I played there for seven days after I got the job! Man, I tore that place up. After that I went with Major Lance, with Monkey Time Records and that created my style. I got my edge so that let people out there who I was as a drummer.

Lamonte McClemore:

Our paths have crossed so many times, Mr. Thompson, from Jet Magazine, they all know you and love you too, and I shot Major Lance as a photographer for Jet and Ebony Magazine. They all talked about you and loved The Chi-Lites.

♪ ♪ ♪

Guest:
Robin Russell of New Birth

Marshall Thompson:

Glad to be back here with the bad New Birth, a group that traveled with us for quite some time, you know, back in the day and we're still doing a lot of things together.

It's a pleasure to have Robin on the line to tell us about what he's doing and the times he came into contact with The Chi-Lites, my group.

It's my pleasure to have you here today, Sir.

Robin Russell:

Well, thank you Marshall. It's my honor. Man, The Chi-Lites, you guys, oh my God, even before I joined New Birth, I knew about The Chi-Lites. I used to hear you guys' records and I never dreamed that I would be hanging out and meeting groups like you guys. It was just always so good when we did shows together. It was always an inspiration because you guys were like a Rock of Gibraltar, as far as R&B/Soul music, so it was my honor whenever that happened. I thank you very much!

Marshall Thompson:

It was a pleasure meeting you all too! You all had the same sound when you were on tour with us. You never lost your sound either; I've made a lot of babies with y'all music, as well. (Laughs)

Robin Russell:

(Laughs) I've heard that! People have said that.

Marshall Thompson:

I created about seven of them off that one record, Wildflower.

Robin Russell:

(Laughs) There's truth to that statement. I'm just happy; it thrills and honors me to know that that song connected with people in such a way; it's very emotional how that connection happened.

I loved those years being with New Birth when we were an eleven or twelve piece unit.

It was a family situation. We were very close; very tight and we were dedicated to what we were doing. Thinking back, I didn't even realize how dedicated we were. It just seemed natural. We knew what we wanted to do; we were on a mission. It was just the thing to do as a group, as a family. This is what we're doing. We're making music. Whatever it takes to keep this thing going, let's do it. It was so much peace and harmony back in those days; in the group, ya' know. It was family for sure.

Marshall Thompson:

You must have had a beautiful time because your music touched a lot of people.

♪ ♪ ♪

Guest:
Howard Hewett

Marshall Thompson:

Good evening. It's a pleasure to be here tonight.

Howard Hewett:

Hi. How are you?

Marshall Thompson:

It's a blessing to have you on, Howard. We go back so many years with Dick Griffey. You are a super, super singer and I always you and loved your voice, and all the people back then; Jodie Whatley, Soul Train and you really put it on through. You're still doing it today! I've been hearing about you from all my friends, Ken Bedford, and them. When I come off the touring myself, I'm hearing about you doing your thang! Every place I get to see you, you're tearing the house down!

Howard Hewett:

Thank you. Thank you. I appreciate that!

Marshall Thompson:

Right on! Me and Don Cornelius were very close, you know, with the Soul Train situation. When Don started here in Chicago he used to tell me about the group, Shalamar. I wanted to see this group so when they came to Chicago, he had them out there at the big arena. I went to see Shalamar, Lakeside, and all of them. I was sitting right there in the front seat and I watched Shalamar do their thing and they just blew me away. I told Don, man you really, really put something together there, buddy! You have a great group there, and I've been following them ever since.

Howard Hewett:

I thank you for that, Marshall. That was the Solar Galaxy of Stars Tour. It was Lakeside, The Whispers, Kerry Lucas, and then the second time we went out it was Dynasty also. We used to have a ball. It was an amazing time and amazing camaraderie with the groups at the time and Solar was into a really, really special thing at that time.

Marshall Thompson:

You were at the Rosemount Arena in Chicago when I saw you. It was packed!

Howard Hewett:

I think the first show I remember doing with The Chi-Lites was when I was doing my solo thing, if I'm not mistaken, Marshall. I think it was in New York somewhere. It was a bunch of groups on the show! I've done so many shows that I can't think of where it was.

Marshall Thompson:

You might have been with me at The Beacon Theater.

Howard Hewett:

I think you're right. Yep.

Marshall Thompson:

You always had a great talent as a solo artist or with the group, you have a great style of voice and when you opened your mouth, you knew it was Howard Hewett singing, and I love you for that!

Howard Hewett:

That was the whole thing about back in the day, it was all about being unique. When it was Stevie, you knew it was Stevie Wonder. When you heard Donny, you knew it was Donny Hathaway. When it was Marvin you knew it, but nowadays you can't tell who's who. Everybody's biting off of everybody.

Marshall Thompson:

Yep, you better believe it! You're right!

♪ ♪ ♪

Guest:
Billy Brown of Ray, Goodman and Brown

Marshall Thompson:

How're you doing there, Brother Bill?

Billy Brown:

Hey Marshall, I'm doing well, thank you.

Marshall Thompson:

Well, welcome to the show. It's a blessing to have you. When I found out you were our guest on the show tonight, I said what an honor. We go back over 40 years.

Billy Brown:

Well it's a blessing to be here on your show with your listeners. Yep, a long time.

Marshall Thompson:

We were on tour together in Indianapolis for Mr. Bell, and Billy Stewart was there. When we left he and his band's bus went off the highway and they passed away. Me, Billy, and Al have been friends ever since, all those years. Al Goodman called me to take his place on an album. We had just been on tour headlining the Cruise Jazz Festival and they had to take off for a while to go cut the album for

Special Lady. I took Eugene, Squirrel, and Red over to Universal Records. That's the first time we'd ever met them at Universal. We went there and stayed for 20 years.

Billy Brown:

We've been together for many years. We managed to stay atop and abreast of what's going on out here in the music scene. We just tried to give people good shows and still sing good music. And that's the thing!

Billy Brown:

Other songs that came out of Polydor were *Inside of You* and *Take It To the Limit*, well actually that came out of a production company owned by Charles Huggins and Melba Moore. We recorded four albums with them, but the *Ray, Goodman and Brown* one was the top selling album out of all the albums we did for Polydor; as a matter of fact we sold about 800 thousand copies. That's our biggest selling album to date!

Guest:
Gerald Alston of The Manhattans

Gerald Alston:

How are you doing, Marshall?

Marshall Thompson:

I got "The Voice" on the show, my man! (Laughs)

Gerald Alston:

(Laughs) Thank you! Well, I could actually sing before I could walk, but I realized it around the 7th or 8th grade when I performed in a talent show. I performed a song by Sam Cooke called *Tennessee Waltz*. It was our homecoming week at school in high school and my performance took everybody by storm. From there I just kept going. I put a band together. I knew then I wanted to keep going but it really, really, really took off when I joined The Manhattans. That's when I knew the time had arrived.

When I first met The Manhattans, they used my sound equipment; I opened the show for them that particular night. They took my name and address and I didn't give it any more thought but the phone kept ringing and ringing that weekend. Unfortunately George Smith had taken sick that weekend and they had to send him home. They flew me down to Dallas and Philip Flood was working in Smittey's place. I watched them for ten days touring with The Supremes and then

I joined the group. It was like, unbelievable. After the rehearsal I started my very first date was the Heavyhitters! We performed in Richmond, Virginia at the Mosque. It was The Dells, The O'Jays, The Spinners, Willie Feast and The Mighty Magnificents, Kool and the Gang, Patti LaBelle and The Bluebelles. That was my debut show!

We got there late; we had all kinds of problems getting there and the promoter wasn't going to let us go on. The Dells were headlining so they went to the promoter and told him, if The Manhattans can't go on after all the trouble they've been through getting here, we're not going on. I'll always remember that. The Dells have always been like that towards us, and they made it possible for us to go on that night. We had to go behind all those people, but that was my beginning.

When I joined The Manhattans, my Uncle, Johnnie Fields – one of the five members of The Blind Boys of Alabama approached me about singing lead for The Soul Stirrers and I said yes, but when the job came through my mother and father had already signed me with The Manhattans. The Soul Stirrers, along with Sam Cooke was my all time mentor. I did a tribute album to him.

Marshall Thompson:

About 34 years ago we started touring together, a lot. We've been up and down that road together! We've done shows where we had to find the promoter to pay us. (Laughs)

Gerald has been a super, super singer. You're one of my favorite.

♪ ♪ ♪

Guests:
Wendell Sawyer and Keith Beaton
of Blue Magic

Marshall Thompson:

How're you doing?

Keith Beaton:

Aw, we're doing good, man. We love you from the bottom of our hearts, and if it wasn't for you, The Chi-Lites, and the Chicago field we wouldn't be here. We love you, Marshall. It was so good to see you in Chicago, I think it was a year ago.

Marshall Thompson:

Right! It's so good to have you on the show tonight.

Keith Beaton:

Well, it's a pleasure to be here.

Wendell Sawyer:

Yes, it is! What's up, Marshall? How've you been man?

Marshall Thompson:

Aye, it's a pleasure to hear you guys' voices.

Keith Beaton:

We've been doing this for over forty years now and to remember the exact moment that we touched bases would be kind of hard but what I can say this. Before we were Blue Magic we were the Shades of Love. It was Vernon Sawyer, Richard Pratt, Keith Beaton and we used to sing The Coldest Days of my Life! I'll never forget that! We always had The Chi-Lites as our idols. Man, we tried to be like you guys as much as we could. But when we did meet, it was like meeting your idols you grew up praising all your life; we were like in shock!

Marshall Thompson:

Well, I'll tell you something about that Blue Magic group because you see, I was the only skinny one in our group, so I could do all the steps you guys did because I was skinny but the other guys had two left feet. (Laughs)

Keith Beaton:

We always loved you because you always looked out for us. But I heard something about you sir. I heard you had 150 suits in your closet, and 300 hats! (Laughs)

Wendell Sawyer:

What I remember about Chicago is that it was cold as hell! It was the Coldest Days of my Life! The wind was blowing and we'd never felt wind like that before. We performed at so many spots together, you know, it's hard to figure out the exact place it was. But I know the shows were some of the greatest. The people left satisfied. The

Chi-Lites did their thing, we did our thing and we put it all on the stage. I started wearing hats because they were wearing hats!

Marshall Thompson:

We had to wear them gansta' hats. (Laughs)

♪ ♪ ♪

Guest:
Gene Chandler-The Duke of Earl

Marshall Thompson:

How're you doing? Good evening.

We have my mentor on tonight. This is fabulous!

Gene Chandler:

Hello. Hello. Hello. I'm just fine.

(Laughs) Well, what an introduction!

I don't know what to say; it's all been said.

Marshall Thompson:

(Laughs) Welcome Gene. You are my mentor.

I know the world should know. I talk about you in every interview I do across the world.

It's a pleasure to have you on the show. I'm glad I could catch up with you to do it. You invite me to your house every year for the 4th of July for a fabulous dinner. Man, we just go crazy over there!

Gene Chandler:

Yep! We always have a good time.

My parents always went to a 4th of July picnic out in in far on the far west side of Chicago and I always loved and sang this song. I don't know why, but it was Danny Boy. At 5 years old I could sing.

47

They asked me to go up on the stage and sing Danny Boy, and as a little kid I knew nothing about being frightened because I sang it around the house all the time; so I just went up there and sung it!

I listened to the songs that my parents played. Once in a while they would have a gathering at the house and of course I was supposed to be in my room asleep, and I wasn't. I'd be peeping through the door listening until I saw someone coming and I'd run and jump in the bed. (Laughs)

But anyway, at their parties they would play these songs by Nat King Cole, Ella Fitzgerald, Frank Sinatra, Tony Bennett, Louie Jordan, Duke Ellington, and that kind of music. I got to learn a lot of those, and then they would take me to the Regal Theater which was about a block from where I lived. I lived close to the corner and the Regal was only a few steps away. They took me around there a few times to see shows. Rather than get a babysitter, they took me. My little feet didn't even touch the floor.

I always remembered Billy Holiday. Whenever she would sing, they never showed her whole body. They would have this round scene on her face and she always had this flower in her hair.

I didn't realize who she was until I got older. It was very exciting to me.

I said, one day I'm going to be up there on that stage, and it did happen!

That was some of the things happening around the Regal Theater before I met Marshall or The Chi-Lites.

I hold the attendance record for the Regal Theater. S. B. Fuller was the owner at the time. He owned a cosmetics company at the time. He bought the Regal Theater and the shopping center. He came to me that week and asked me what I was doing with my money. The

Regal was very successful that week, not only in attendance but he'd made $50,000 in concessions and that was a big deal. He was trying to advise me about my money.

♪ ♪ ♪

Guest:
Lloyd Price

Lloyd Price:

With a #1 record, The Chi-Lites are one of my favorite groups. What a perfect group that was. We have a lot of friends back here that love Marshall, love The Chi-Lites and love Carl Davis. Chicago is kind of the center of this thing we call Blues, and it was no question about it. If you went to Chicago that's where you met all the great talent! Marshall Thompson, Carl Davis, and Gus Redmond put a stamp on it for America, and the rest of the world. It was more than a pleasure when Marshall and The Chi-Lites was #1 around the world. I'd met Marshall a long time before that. They went on and lit up the world as a group and that made me more than happy.

Marshall Thompson:

Thank you. And I am still honored to be doing this, as the Last Man Standing, Mr. Personality.

Lloyd Price:

I started learning and making a commitment to music as early as seven years old. My mother had a sandwich shop and a juke box in there. Back then there was only 10 sides on the jukebox, 20 songs and each one cost a nickel to play. I started learning songs from artists like Camille Howard, Roy Milton of the Lincoln Brothers, Anna

Lauren, Paul Gaitan, Charles Brown, Nat King Cole. I learned all of their songs! I mean these were the real roots of how this music began. This like in my teen years. The first black jockey I recognized on the radio was a guy named Okie, Dokie. He really got me hooked in the business. He came on for Maxwell coffee and he'd say, Lawdy Miss Clawdy, eat your mother's home cooked pies and drink Maxwell coffee! (Laughs) I heard Lawdy, Miss Clawdy out of everything he said. I was wondering why that was so outstanding and present in my mind because it played all week but wasn't nobody talking about the Lord until Sunday! That really got my attention because that was on a Tuesday. I was about 13 or 14 and he continuously grew as a popular figure on the air. He really became a Personality. As he became bigger, I became more popular with the little band I had in a town call Kenna, Louisiana. The street I grew up on was named after me, Lloyd Price Avenue. It's how Lawdy, Miss Clawdy came about. It was 323 Butler Street in Kenna. I was told about a guy coming from California looking for talent. Fats Domino had just had a hit, They Call Me the Fat Man, and they wanted somebody younger than Fats. I played the song for them; they got Fats on the piano. We did two takes with no playbacks. I was scared to death. He gave me $50, and I had never seen a fifty dollar bill before. Then I went home.

Marshall Thompson:

(Laughs) Wow.

Lloyd Price:

About three or four weeks later my brother came to me talking about he keeps hearing this song on the radio with Oakey Smith, and the guy keeps playing this song called Lawdy, Miss Clawdy by a kid from Kenna named Lloyd Price. He asked, is that you? I had never heard myself on the radio so I couldn't tell whether it was me or not! I said, let's wait until the record is over and hear what he's say's. So that's how it got started. It's been recorded 178 times by some of the biggest rock stars in the world, beginning with Fats Domino, The Beatles, Elvis Presley, etc. You name them they have recorded it!

♪ ♪ ♪

Guest:
Stan Mosley

Marshall Thompson:

A pleasant good evening. How're doing, very talented brother?

Stan Mosley:

I'm blessed above and beyond anything I could ever hope for or imagine.

Marshall Thompson:

Right On! It's a very good pleasure to have you on tonight.

Stan Mosley:

It's a pleasure to be on here with you, man. I've been looking forward to this all week. And here I am. (Laughs)

Marshall Thompson:

(Laughs) We're going to let our listeners know all about you and what you're doing.

Stan Mosley:

Well, first of all anybody that grew up in Chicago belonged to somebody's church, and you know as well as I do Marshall, that there was some slammin' music in the church. (Laughs) Everybody could pretty much get down with the choirs.

Marshall Thompson:

Definitely.

Stan Mosley:

My love for the music really began when I would see cats like Jackie Wilson, Sam Cooke, and Wilson Pickett on the Ed Sullivan Show. I was a very, very young kid and I think it came on every Sunday around 6 or 7 o'clock, but we got an opportunity to see our people on a huge platform, a huge stage. You're talking about tv was black and white back then and you got a chance to see them shining. That just touched me in a very, very unique way. I'll never forget it.

My mother told me one time that I used to stand on the front porch with the water hose like it was a microphone singing, ya' know. (Laughs)

She said if I wasn't imitating Wilson Pickett, I was imitating Elvis Presly, so hey, ya' know. (Laughs)

I've been doing this for a long time and I have enjoyed doing it.

I was in the Army too and have been around the world two or three times.

Musically as a youth I had some friends that lived there on the block with me. We used to mess around listening to the Supremes, The Miracles, The Temptations and The Four Tops. We would sit on the front porch in the evenings, I mean every evening and try to harmonize with each other. None of us could sing. (Laughs)

We couldn't sing a lick but we would get together and do that. I kinda of found out that the more we did it, the better we became. We just kept singing and it became fun. That's when I found out I sound something special. At least that's what I thought and wanted to believe. My mother told me it was used as something constructive;

as a tool to keep us out of trouble by keeping us right there together, singing in the neighborhood.

The first time I saw The Chi-Lites, I believe it was on Halsted for Operation Push.

They had The Chi-Lites down, Tyrone Davis, The Autistics, they had everybody from Brunswick and the Chi-Sound family down there. I'll never forget, The Chi-Lites just came out there and blew the roof off of it! They were moving so fast I thought I saw five of them on stage. (Laughs)

Marshall Thompson:

(Laughs) I remember that day. That was the first time we were at the amphitheater on Halsted. When we came back the second time we had Michael Jackson and Motown and them in there, but the first time when you went we had strictly Jesse Jackson. Operation Push brought us in there.

Stan Mosley:

That's who I got the tickets from, Jesse Jackson.

THE BEGINNING.

Soulfully Yours,
Soul School Music® on TRIBE Family Channel™

Afterword

by Dr. Marshall Thompson

First, I'd like to start off by thanking all the wonderful people for making this book series possible, based on the radio show Soul School Music, that Beverly Black Johnson and I co-hosted together. There are too many to name individually. My good buddy Dr. Otis Williams summed it all up in the Foreword for which I am eternally grateful. I've always looked up to him and The Temptations.

Daisy Brown has been a real sister and friend for over fifty years, and I am proud to say we are still making moves together. She has helped The Chi-Lites to get where we are.

The guys who are with me in spirit, Eugene Record, Robert "Squirrel" Lester and Creadel "Red" Jones, and I have been truly blessed through so many years of ups and downs. I know they are smiling upon me, saying "We did it!" and "Keep going!" That keeps me going!

I am now 81 years young and have celebrated a musical career filled with some fascinating times, shared with a lot of amazing people.

I hope you'll enjoy these snippets from those good times.

I come from a long line of jazz singers and musicians on both parents' sides of my family. Many played with the likes of Louis Armstrong and some real greats in the business. I love all types of music, but Soul music is what resonates in my spirit.

These interviews capture times past that are indescribable. We have all been truly blessed.

Lastly, I'd like to thank my loving family, for all the time they've sacrificed through the years so that as an entertainer, I could do what I do. Now we can enjoy the fruits together.

~ Dr. Marshall Thompson,
The Last Man Standing of The Chi-Lites.

About The Chi-Lites

It started in 1959 when Marshall Thompson formed a vocal group called the "Hi-Lights" in his hometown of Chicago with fellow members Eugene Record, Robert Lester and Creadel "Red" Jones. After releasing several singles on local labels, the group changed their name in 1964 to "Marshall & The Chi-Lites". By the time the group changed their name to The Chi-Lites in 1969 they were signed by Nat Tarnopol and Carl Davis to Brunswick Records, where they would soon become international superstars.

Between 1969 and 1974, The Chi-Lites scored eleven Top Ten singles on the Billboard R&B charts, with hits like "Have You Seen Her", "Give It Away", "(For God's Sake) Give More Power To The People", "Are You My Woman (Tell Me So)", "A Letter To Myself", "The Coldest Days of My Life", "Stoned Out Of My Mind", "Oh Girl" and thirty seven other Billboard charted singles throughout their career. During the 1970's The Chi-Lites were featured on television shows such as Soul Train, American Bandstand, The Midnight Special, Sammy and Company, the BBC's Top of the Pops, and the very popular Flip Wilson Show, where they debuted their #1 pop smash "Oh Girl". All of The Chi-Lites' hits were written or co-written by lead singer Eugene Record, who would also become Brunswick's Vice President of A&R.

In 2000, BMI named "Oh Girl" by The Chi-Lites the 36th most popular song of the 20th century. That same year The Chi-Lites were inducted into the Rhythm & Blues Hall Of Fame followed by their induction into Vocal Groups Hall Of Fame in 2004. The Chi-Lites have also appeared on screen in the 1996 feature film "Original Gangsters" with Fred Williams, Jim Brown, Pam Grier, and Richard Roundtree, as well as the 2003 docu/movie "Only The Strong Survive" by Miramax films.

Grammy-winning audio engineer Bruce Swedien insists that when he recorded Michael Jackson's vocals for the "Off The Wall" and "Thriller" albums, he used the same techniques he developed with The Chi-Lites in the early 1970s. In addition to being featured in many films, television shows and commercials, the recordings of The Chi-Lites have been sampled by artists such as Jay-Z, K. Michelle, American Idol winner Fantasia and Beyonce, who sampled The Chi-Lites to create the Grammy winning smash "Crazy In Love". In 2021, the Chi-Lites were honored with a star on the Hollywood Walk of Fame and in 2022 Marshall Thompson began a residency at Duomo inside The Rio Hotel and Casino.

Now, Dr. Marshall Thompson, since December 4, 2022, has received an Honorary Doctorate in Humane Letters and the Presidential Medal of Freedom for all The Chi-Lites' endeavors.

About Beverly Black Johnson

Beverly Black Johnson hails from San Francisco, CA.

She is the CEO and Founder of Gumbo for the Soul International, the umbrella of Gumbo for the Soul Publications est. 2003, and Gumbo for the Soul Literacy Program, a 501c(4) Literacy Initiative.

Through her company she gives back to the community by publishing and giving away books primarily focusing on health and wellness. In 2005 the imprint debuted with the 2X literary award-winning anthology Gumbo for the Soul: The Recipe for Literacy in the Black Community, which garnered the support of Tavis Smiley. "'Gumbo for the Soul' dares to call it like it is.

This serving of Gumbo is a must-read for every parent, teacher, mentor and all who believe it is important that our children can read and comprehend the English language." -Tavis Smiley, Author, Television, Radio Host Beverly's speaking subjects are geared towards fostering literacy, self-empowerment, and inspiration within the scope of education, health and wellness, suicide prevention, and overcoming drug addiction.

She is available for your organizational or community events. She can be reached via her company website and email address below.

gumboforthesoulinternational@gmail.com

www.gumboforthesoulinternational.com

"Show business is 90% business; 10% show!"

Dr. Marshall Thompson of The Chi-Lites

Glossary of Guests by Seasons

Book 1 - Season One 2016:

Patryce "Choc'Let" Banks, Brenda Lee Eager,
and Gary Dennis Hines.
Sonny Turner
Brenda Lee Eager
Little Anthony of Little Anthony and The Imperials
Lamont McClemore of The Fifth Dimension.
Robin Russell of New Birth
Howard Hewett
Billy Brown of Ray, Goodman and Brown
Gerald Alston of The Manhattans
Wendell Sawyer and Keith Beaton of Blue Magic
Gene Chandler-The Duke of Earl
Lloyd Price
Stan Mosley

Book Release Date: September 2023

Book 2 - Season Two 2017:

William Hart of The Delfonics
Bobbi Humphrey
Chris Jasper of Isley Jasper Isley
Stan Alston of The Main Ingredient
Jerome Jackson, Don Black and Larry Moore
of The Main Ingredient
William "Smoke" Howard of The Ebony's
Cliff Perkins of Soul Generation
Skip Mahoney of The Casuals
Kevin Owens -Luther Vandross back-up singer
of 30 years.
David Banks of Enchantment
The Notations
The Spindles
The Unifics
Keith Jackson of The Jackson Family
The Floaters
The Persuaders
The Young Senators
EJ Johnson of Enchantment
Fannie Brown and Jimmie Lee Moore, Bass Player
with The JB's, honoring James Brown
Cliff Perkins formerly of Curtom/Gemigo Records
honoring Curtis Mayfield

Book Release Date: October 2023

Book 3 - Season Three 2018:

Bloodstone
Khalilah Ali (former wife of Ali)
honoring Muhammed Ali
Lenny Williams (Tower of Power)
Force MD's
Randall Bostick of Rick James Stone City Band
honoring Teena Marie
Cheryl Cooley of Klymaxx
Otis Williams of The Temptations
Reginald Haynes of The Escorts
Stan Alston of The Main Ingredient
The Lovelights
honoring Phyllis Hyman
Keith Jackson honoring Joe Jackson
Rick James' Stone City Band honoring Rick James
Marshall Thompson 76th birthday
with The Chi-Lites family
Keith Jackson honoring Michael Jackson and
Michael Henderson honoring Aretha Franklin
Katina Anderson (BB King's Granddaughter) &
Tomiko Dixon (Willie Dixon's Granddaughter)
honoring B.B. King's birthday
Raynae Robinson -Ray Charles' daughter, and
Patricia Maltz, manager of Sheila Raye Charles,
honoring Ray Charles and Sheila Raye Charles

Book Release Date: December 2023

Book 4 - Season Four 2019:

David Banks of Enchantment and The Chi-Lites
family honoring Larry Cunningham of The Floaters
Tawatha Agee (Mtume)
Deniece "Niecy" Williams
and surprise caller Dr. Otis Williams
Charles Wright, Founder and leader of the
legendary Watts 103rd Street Rhythm Band
Guest Speech Thomas of Arrested Development
Charles Chuck Barksdale of The Dells
with Cliff Perkins and Stan Alston
Honoring Willie Ford of The Dramatics

Book Release Date: February 2024

Book 5 - Season Five 2019:

Fred & Diana Simon, and Charles Jackson
of The Lost Generation and surprise caller
Gus Redmond
Black Ivory
The Ohio Players' drummer
James Diamond Williams
George Kerr
The Detroit Emeralds (James Mitchell, Jr..
Dwayne Loc Lomaz, Lavel Jackson,
Eddie Cameron)
The Ladies of Skyy
Henry Fambrough of The Spinners

Book Release Date: April 2024

Book 6 - Season Six 2020:

The Chi-Lites 61st Anniversary Celebration
Otis Williams/The Temptations Book Celebration
The Bluenotes Honoring Trudy Melvin
The Intruders
Honoring Legends Little Richard and Betty Wright
Bobby Brooks Wilson (Son of Jackie Wilson)
honoring Jackie "Mr. Excitement" Wilson's
86th bEarthday
The Manhattans featuring Gerald Alston
Billy Brown of Ray, Goodman, and Brown
Lenny Williams
Billy Griffin (The Miracles)
Ray Parker, Jr.
Lenny Williams
The Whispers
The Drells (Archie Bell and The Drells)
honoring The Chi-Lites' own, Eugene Record
Archie Bell (Archie Bell and The Drells)

Book Release Date: June 2024

CORPORATE PLATINUM SPONSORS

In Loving Memory of
Willie George Adams
1945 – 2022

https://gordavi.com

https://hummingbirdandyellowrose.com

www.incarceratedlivesmatter.org

www.Take20ForLife.com

Suicide Prevention Organization | Take 20 Minutes,
it could save your life!

https://tnurbanoutdoors.org/

GOLD SPONSORS:

The Isaac Lindsey Network
Ray Parker, Jr.
Clyde Gambrell, Sr.
Alan T. Black
Bette Travis
Albert Jordan, Jr.
Lori LJ Johnson
The LJ Today Show
Adrian Ingram
J. Elliot Howard
Michele A. Barard LLC
Jeff McKinney
Mr/Mrs. Timothy & Alma Williams

www.ingramcontent.com/pod-product-compliance
Lightning Source LLC
Chambersburg PA
CBHW060351130626
46553CB00003B/1177